Encountering

Christmas

Encountering
Christmas

CAROLYN J SWEERS

Sweers
sweers@wi.rr.com
414 291 5981

ENCOUNTERING CHRISTMAS

This book is written to provide information and motivation to readers. Its purpose is not to render any type of psychological, legal, or professional advice of any kind. The content is the sole opinion and expression of the author, and not necessarily that of the publisher.

ISBN   978-1-949746-95-2   (Paperback)
ISBN   978-1-949746-96-9   (Digital)

Lettra Press books may be ordered through booksellers or by contacting:

Lettra Press LLC
18229 E 52nd Ave.
Denver City, CO 80249
1 303 586 1431 | info@lettrapress.com
www.lettrapress.com

CONTENTS

PREFACE

The stories of Christmas are familiar and that can be a problem.

I grew up with the Christmas stories. I participated in Sunday School Christmas programs. I learned the carols. But it was not until I was drawn back to church after a ten-year absence, that I began to experience the shock value of the Christmas stories with their amazing, impossible seeming claim, that God, the Creator of the Universe, had appeared on earth, in human form.

I remember vividly the morning after attending my first Midnight Mass at the Cathedral of St. John the Evangelist in Milwaukee. I was on the train, going to Chicago to spend the day with friends. In my still altered mental state, from the glorious event of the night before, I suddenly thought of the Red Queen's conversation with Alice in Louis Carroll's <u>Through the Looking Glass</u>. The topic was "impossible things" and the importance of believing them; a task that required considerable practice. In fact, the Queen said, she herself had gotten so good at it that she once believed several impossible things "before breakfast". How many "impossible things" there were in the Christmas stories, I then realized: angel appearances, mysterious births, and the most "impossible" of all, that God had appeared in human form. Believing these might, in fact, take a bit of practice.

The Church provides a sort of "practice" period for Christmas. It is called Advent. It is a time of quiet expectancy when there are more hours of dark than there is of light in the region where I live. It is a time of preparation. It is a time of letting go: a letting-go of what is most familiar about Christmas so that the wondrous Nativity stories may expand our awareness of what is possible for ourselves and for the world.

PROLOGUE

(from Chapter 1 of the Gospel of John)

In the beginning was the Word
and the Word was with God,
and the Word was God.

And the light shown in the darkness;
and the darkness comprehended it not.

The true Light...was in the world,
and the word was made by him,
and the world knew him not.

But the time came that
the Word was made flesh,
and dwelt among us,
and we beheld His glory.

Out of the ageless Silence,
The womb of words and work,
this WORD
started toward us
before what would be us
took flesh and grew.
Was it this WORD
for which our eyes
and ears
were made?

HOW TO PREPARE FOR CHRISTMAS?

Practice believing impossible things.

Read the Nativity Stories.
Notice how "impossible" they are.
There are angels,
mysterious births,
a variety of humans who have "other wordily" encounters.
There is the "cosmic" claim
that God appeared
in human form.

**The Christmas stories
are just one "Impossible" thing
after another,
as you will soon see.**

To prepare for Christmas,
to truly prepare,
become intentionally empty,
intentionally receptive.
Hear the stories,
as if
for the very first time.
How startling
that would
be.

The challenge is to find ourselves
in these old stories,
find our fits and starts,
our fears,
our presumption.
The challenge is to find in those stories
the place
where we lie hidden
waiting
for the birthing God
who keeps drawing
near.

Who are we....really?
Is a question
some philosophers ask.

The answer of Christmas?

We are offspring of Divinity
worth a Visit
to remind us.

The Babe resembles us
as we are
and could become.

Carolyn J Sweers

THE STORIES OF CHRISTMAS

**When it comes to scripture
we have two basic and quite different choices.**
One choice is to try to understand scripture
and to accept it or reject it depending on
whether it "makes sense".
But a second way
is to let the passages draw us in,
to master, at least temporarily, our awareness.
Let us dare
to do the second.

Think of these stories as a series of doors,
any one of which,
if entered,
plunges one into
a heart quickening wonder.

THE NATIVITY STORIES

Zacharias and Elisabeth

Mary

Joseph

The Birth of Jesus

The Magi

Herod

The Shepherds.

THE FIRST CHRISTMAS

Matthew, the Gospel writer,
tells it like this.

When Mary was espoused to Joseph,
a quite normal arrangement
for the times,
before they came together ("had sex", is what I think is meant)
she was found with child.
That, too, is not all that unusual.
But wait.
Are your ready for the next part?
Of course you're not
and that is the point.
It will take something you're not ever ready for
to shake you into
God awareness.
"She was found with child of the Holy Ghost."
Mathew did not say how that came about
but Luke, another Gospel writer, did.
But first,
a long and very different story
though intimately connected
to the main event.

ZACHARIAS

ZACHARIAS. In the days of Herod, the king of Judea, there was a certain priest named Zacharias who was married to Elisabeth. They were both righteous people, and kept all the commandments of God. The great disappointment of their lives was that they had no children. Elisabeth was barren and they were both quite old ("stricken in years"). It came to pass, that while Zacharias was on priestly duty, offering incense in the inner sanctum of the temple, there appeared to him an angel of the Lord standing on the right side of the altar of incense. When Zacharias saw the angel, he was troubled and "fear fell upon him". But the angel told him not to be afraid. His prayer had been answered. He and his wife Elisabeth were going to have a son whom they were to name John. The angel went on to describe how important John's work would be. It was John, later known as the "Baptist" who would announce the coming arrival of the Savior and would recognize him when he saw him.

When Zacharias had heard all this, he doubted that it could be true. He said to the angel, "How can this be? Both my wife and I are old." To this the angel replied, quite forcefully, "I am Gabriel, that stands in the presence of God and was sent here, by God, to give you this good news ("glad tidings"). And because you have doubted this, you will be struck dumb, unable to speak, until the things I predicted have happened."

So, when Zacharias emerged from the temple to bless the people, people who had been waiting for what had seemed to be an unusually long time, the people could see right away that something dramatic had happened to Zacharias. He seemed to have seen a vision...and he could not speak. He was physically incapable of communicating what he had seen or heard.

And so, Zacharias went home and after some days had passed, Elisabeth became pregnant and went into seclusion for 5 months. (Luke 1:5-14, KJV)

ZACHARIAS

Here is the way Luke introduces us
to the improbable.
He tells the story of a certain priest named Zacharias
who was married to Elisabeth.
They were both good people:
"righteous before God", Luke said,
which, as a matter of fact,
is not all that easy to do.
But, despite how good they were,
how consistently they have followed all of God's commands
(not just the ones they liked),
their heart's desire was for a child.
That had not happened.
Elisabeth was barren
and now the couple was quite old.
("Well stricken in years" is the King James phrase.)
"And it came to pass…"
(I don't know about you
but I love that phrase.
Moves humans out from
the center of actions.)
"And it came to pass…"
as if it just happened.
No big deal.
But when that "came to pass" phrase turns up,
it really means,
Pay close attention.
You may not think you can believe what comes next,
but please try to!

Let us remember Zacharias,
who one day, as was his job,
went into the inner sanctuary to light some incense.
Often, even to the devout,
God can seem more memory than Presence.
But this day, this particular day,
the day that Zacharias went in,
there was an angel
Something not even a priest expected.
But there he was!
And what did the angel say?
No new commandment.
No, it seemed to be this angel's job to make a birth
announcement.
"You are going to be a father, Zacharias"
That is what the angel said.
Nothing any angel could have said could have evoked such fear,
such dread, such crazy hope in the heart of that old man.
Zacharias,
presumably no stranger to awe
having entered the "Holy of Holies" numerous times,
when he saw the angel,
he was troubled.
(Wouldn't you be?
If you weren't afraid, it was probably not really an angel
you saw.
I owe this insight to the poet Rilke.)
"Fear fell upon him", Luke says.
This is way more than just trembling and shaking.
Something seemed to come over him:
fear like a force.

Carolyn J Sweers

But the angel said to Zacharias,
(that word "but" seems to calm the situation slightly...
a little pause before the really amazing part.
More amazing than an angel showing up?)

The angel said unto him, "Fear not, Zacharias:
(easy enough for an angel to say)
for thy prayer is heard: and thy wife Elisabeth shall bear thee a son,
and thou shalt call his name John.
But that's not all, said this somewhat loquacious angel,
"You and a lot of other people are going to be very happy,
"rejoicingly" happy, as a matter of fact.
This child, this long awaited, improbable child
(the angel did not say "improbable",
he did not need to.)
this long-awaited child "shall be great in the sight of the Lord."
"He shall drink neither wine nor strong drink,
lest people think he is drunk
when he speaks.
He shall be filled with the Holy Ghost,
even from his mother's womb."
(The importance of that detail comes a bit later.)

In fact, continued the talkative angel,
he will remind people of the famous old prophet, Elias
able to "turn the hearts of fathers to the children, and the
disobedient to the wisdom of the just; to make ready a people
prepared for the Lord."
Well, Zacharias, what do you think of THAT?
Not very much, as it turns out.
Maybe Zacharias was just in a daze,
trying desperately
to hold onto a semblance of sanity.
Luke says that Zacharias doubted that what the angel said was
going to happen.
"Whereby shall I know this?", Zacharias asked.
("Dude! you were just told that by an angel, for God's sake.")

Zacharias, still trapped in his muttering, stuttering way of being
said that both he and his wife were old:
"stricken with years".
Zacharias may not have been a stranger to awe
but he wasn't so good at grasping the miraculous,
a rather common human trait, to be fair to the priest.
The angel answered him, not something angels always do,
but this one, as if provoked by the old man's excuses,
said "I am Gabriel!"
(When an angel tells you his name,
things have really gotten serious.)

The angel said: "I am Gabriel. I stand in the presence of God.
I was sent to bring you this great news,
and you doubted.
How dare you!
How dare you question God, whose messenger I am!
Because you doubted, from this moment on you are not going
to be able to talk.
That's right.
Not one word.
You will have to remain silent
until the birth happens.
You will have to be silent from now until then
because you did not believe my words."

**Moral of this part of the story:
never a good idea to doubt an angel.**

Meanwhile,
outside the temple
there was a crowd
waiting for a blessing from the priest.
They had waited so long
they were beginning to wonder
if something had happened
to keep the priest so long inside?

Had he fallen down dead
or taken ill?

Finally, Zacharias did come out,
with a dazed look on his face.
It was obvious he wanted to tell them something.
They saw his mouth form words,
but no sound came out.
They saw him struggling to turn thoughts into words
but his efforts
were in vain.
Something had happened!
The crowd sensed it immediately,
They did not know,
nor could they have guessed
what had happened.
But just seeing old Zacharias's face
was itself a kind of blessing.

Carolyn J Sweers

Luke said that when Zacharias's time of temple duty was up, he
went home
and "in due course"
(presumably after some sex)
his wife got pregnant.
Much of this story is mysterious
but not who had fathered John.

Zacharias, chastened and speechless,
potent with the angel's words,
fathered a son, whose name was John.

But wait
There's more!
(How's your believing impossible things practice going?)

MARY

MARY: Six months after Gabriel had appeared to Zacharias, he was sent by God to a city in Galilee, named Nazareth. He was sent to a virgin who was engaged to a man named Joseph. The virgin's name was Mary. When Gabriel greeted her, he said "Hail, thou that art highly favored, the Lord is with thee: blessed art thou among women." When Mary saw the angel, she was troubled and tried to figure out what was going on. ("cast in her mind what manner of salutation this should be.") Gabriel, noticing her troubled perplexity, said, "Fear not, Mary: for thou hast found favor with God. And behold, thou shalt conceive in thy womb, and bring forth a son, and shalt call his name JESUS. He shall be great, and shall be called the Son of the Highest: and the Lord God shall give unto him the throne of his father David: and he shall reign over the house of Jacob forever; and of his kingdom there shall be no end."

To all this, Mary replied: "How shall this be, seeing I know not a man?"

Gabriel's answer? "The Holy Ghost shall come upon thee, and the power of the Highest shall overshadow thee: therefore also that holy thing which shall be born of thee shall be called the Son of God." And [by the way], your cousin Elisabeth has conceived a son in her old age and she, who was called barren, has been pregnant for six months. For with God nothing shall be impossible."

When Mary heard these words, she said "Behold the handmaid of the Lord; be it unto me according to thy word." And the angel departed from her." (Luke 1:26-38, KJV)

MARY

Gabriel had another birth announcement to deliver;
six months after the one to Zacharias.
This time Gabriel was sent to a woman
and met with more success.
(I will try not to make too much
of that detail.)
This time the angel may have brushed up on communication
skills with humans.
He greeted Mary by name,
and with a very complementary address:
"Hail, thou art highly favored.
The Lord is with thee:
blessed are thou among women."
(How's that for an opening line!)
Hard to think
Mary was not
just a little bit flattered,
wouldn't you be?
Though when this sort of message is delivered by an angel,
it may seem
a bit scary.

But notice.
Mary did not freak out.
She seems to have been a composed,
receptive,
"together" young woman
but she was "troubled",
Luke reported.
Not afraid, really,
but "troubled"
which would seem to be an appropriate response
when confronted
by an angel.
Mary was troubled and "cast in her mind what manner of
salutation this should be."
Not the sort of opening line she could have expected,
let alone know its meaning.
No category in her mind
into which
such a salutation
would fit.
But the angel, as if sensing the thoughts and feelings
coursing beneath a calm exterior, said:
"fear not, Mary: for you have found favor with God".

After the greeting, and after assuring Mary that she has nothing
to fear,
Gabriel began to give details:
"You will become pregnant and give birth to a son, a son you
are to name Jesus."
So far, nothing all that surprising.
Mary was engaged to Joseph, after all.
And expected (hoped) that at some point
she would give birth
to a son.
Though even in her fondest, future mother dreams
could she have imagined what the angel had predicted.
The child would not only be great
(isn't that most mother's hope?),
he will be called "son of the Highest",
and God will give him the throne of his ancestor David.
He will become the kind of ruler
whose kingdom will be
what **God** intends.

At this point, Mary who had been pondering all this,
asked what seemed to be an obvious question:
"How can this be, seeing I know not a man
that I am a virgin still?"
The angel replied:
"This is to be a different kind of conception
than the world has ever known.
The Holy Ghost will come and impregnate you."
Yes, dear reader, this is one of those impossible things
to try to believe
before breakfast.

Stop, just stop at least for a moment.
Try to imagine what it must have been like
to be told
"You are going to give birth—to God!"
If that possibility and all its earth shattering,
history shaping power
does not grab you
and move you toward wonder,
better stop reading.
But if you are stirred,
even a little,
by the momentousness of what Luke described,
linger here
and see what birth
might be waiting
for YOU!

Let us praise, if we dare,
Gabriel,
herald of improbable births.

"Your cousin Elisabeth," Gabriel continued,
"has conceived a child in her old age."
A season of miracles
has just gotten
underway.
In the very next line of the Angel's message,
comes what seems to be the point of it all:
"With God
nothing shall be
impossible."

So, dear humans.
Don't be too quick to think you have things all figured out.
What you can't quite imagine,
what does not "fit" with your experience,
maybe, just maybe,
is God
at work.

Mary's response, so unlike what ours usually is,
has echoed down the years as a model of devotion:

And Mary said, (Luke 1:46-48) **My soul doth magnify the Lord,
And my spirit hath rejoiced in God my Savior.
For he hath regarded the low estate of his handmaiden:
for, behold, from henceforth
all generations
shall call me blessed.**

And they have!

And with that simple assent of Mary's,
the very center of human history was broken into,
impregnated
with
the coming
of God.

MARY VISITS ELISABETH

"Mary arose in those days, and went into the hill country with haste and entered the house of Zacharias, and saluted Elisabeth. And it came to pass, that, when Elisabeth heard the salutation of Mary, the babe leaped in her womb; and Elisabeth was filled with the Holy Ghost: And she spoke out with a loud voice, and said, "Blessed art thou among women, and blessed is the fruit of thy womb. And whence is this to me, that the mother of my Lord should come to me? For lo, as soon as the voice of thy salutation sounded in mine ears, the babe leaped in my womb for joy." (Luke 1:39-44, 56, KJV)

Will the wonders never cease?

Let us hope not!

JOSEPH

Meanwhile,
back at the human,
what about Joseph
to whom
Mary was engaged?
(Matthew 1: 19-21,24)
Joseph was a practical man,
a carpenter who knew how to make things.
He, and the things he made,
were solid,
upright,
what girl could do better.
How did Joseph take Mary's news?
To find out the answer,
we have to go back
to Matthew's account.
Joseph, practical Joseph, probably not given to flights of
imagination
(though that is conjecture)
experienced a moment which many an engaged man has
feared.
His intended was pregnant, but not by him.
A cuckolded carpenter, he might have thought,
but not for long.

While Joseph was still deciding what to do
in these now changed circumstances
(little did he know the full extent of the change)
an angel came to him in a dream.

(One never knows when or how an angel will turn up.)

The angel that appeared to Joseph in a dream
told him what had been conceived in Mary
was the work of the Holy Spirit.
Not something a wide-awake Joseph
might have taken as true.
But dreams are filled with the unexpected.
When Joseph got the dream message
that Mary's pregnancy was of cosmic origin,
a part of an ancient plan,
he did not doubt,
he did not question.
Joseph believed
and he knew what to do.
He married Mary.

Joseph believed and consented
to do his part.
"Be it done to me as You willed,"
he might have said,
to God.
Joseph believed and consented to do his part.
He prepared a place,
a life,
a home
for the coming
of the Lord.

(Dare we do less?)

THE BIRTH OF JESUS

"And it came to pass in those days, that there went out a decree from Caesar Augustus that all the world should be taxed....and all went to be taxed, every one into his own city. And Joseph also went up from Galilee...unto the city of David, which is called Bethlehem; (because he was of the house and lineage of David) to be taxed with Mary his espoused wife, being great with child. And while they were there, the days were accomplished that she should be delivered. And she brought forth her firstborn son, and wrapped him in swaddling clothes, and laid him in a manger; because there was no room for them in the inn." (LUKE 2:1-7, KJV)

VISIT OF THE MAGI

When Jesus was born in Bethlehem in the days of Herod the king, there came wise men from the east to Jerusalem, saying "Where is he that is born King of the Jews? For we have seen his star in the east, and are come to worship him. After an audience with Herod, who was very interested in what they had to say, they went out and there was the star which they had seen in the east and the star led them to the place where the young child was. When they came to the house, they saw the young child with Mary his mother and fell down, and worshipped him: and when they had opened their treasures, they presented him with gifts: gold, and frankincense, and myrrh. But they did not return to Herod, as they had promised. An angel, appearing to them in a dream, warned them against returning to Herod, and so they took a different route back to their own country. (Matthew 2:1-2, 11, KJV)

WISE MEN

The longest journey,
it would seem,
was the one
the wise men took.

In the words of T.S. Eliot
('Journey of the Magi')
'A cold coming we had of it,
Just the worst time of the year
For a journey, and such a long journey:
The ways deep and the weather sharp.'

It was not the first journey
these wise men
would have made.
They had already made a journey toward wisdom
and that way is long
and subject to
hazards.

But this journey was beyond all that...
—a journey into hardship
—a journey into the dark and cold
—a destination not certain in the usual ways.

So why did they do it?

Conjecture is that the Magi
were astrologers of the most sophisticated kind;
skilled at reading sky patterns
and translating what they saw
into guidance for the lives
of earth bound humans.

What these wise men saw one night,
was so astonishing
it drew them up and out
of the comfortable
and familiar.

They made a long journey
following a star
to the place where there was a birth
SO momentous,
even the heavens
blazed in witness.

I said the wise men had the longest journey,
physically perhaps,
but was it a longer journey than the one Mary made?
Or Joseph?
Or even Zacharias?

It is always a long journey
to know,
and consent to,
the inscrutable
but compelling
ways of the Lord.

HEROD

"Herod was king of Judea at the time these events took place. When word reached him that wise men had come asking "Where is he that is born King of the Jews?" Herod grew concerned. Here was what seemed to be a major threat to his power. Herod consulted the Jewish priests and scribes to determine where, according to the prophecies of their tradition, such a King would be born. He was told: Bethlehem in Judea. Herod then had the wise men brought to him.

He wanted to know precisely when the star had appeared and, because he himself wanted to find the child, but not for worship purposes, even though that is what he said, he told the wise men to come back after they had found the child so that he too could pay homage. The wise men left, but they never returned to Herod because, in a dream, they had been warned by an angel, to stay away from the palace and to go home a different way. After a short time had passed, Herod realized the wise men were not coming back and got very angry ("exceeding wroth") and took matters into his own hands and ordered that every boy child, under the age of 2, who had been born in the region of Bethlehem, should be slaughtered. This event is referred to as "Herod's slaughter of the innocents." Many families were left grieving at this atrocity; but the child Herod sought to kill was living safely, in Egypt. (Matthew 2:3-8, 16, KJV)

HEROD AND THE WISE MEN

There were other players in the story.
There was Herod...a king,
a holder of great but tenuous power.
Word reached him that wise men had arrived,
distinguished travelers from the East,
and they had come with a question:
"Where is he that is born King of the Jews?"
They said a bright star
had brought the news
and led them forth.

When news of a possible new King
for the always resentful
restless
Jewish population
reached Herod,
he was filled with fear
but he dared not show it;
dared now show how much
he knew he might lose.
Herod put on a show of courteous bravery.
He summoned the wise men.

Herod knew that his own birth
had not been announced with cosmic signs,
nor had any of the births
of any other king
he knew.
This birth had to be
extraordinary.

A rare new star.
A cosmic portent.
As if the universe itself were giving birth.
Which did not mean
it couldn't be stopped.
(Or so Herod thought.)

When Herod heard the news of a possible new king
for the lands
he thought
he ruled,
he summoned all the politeness
he thought appropriate.
He pretended to be both curious
and respectful.
Herod said to the wise men:
"Go, and search diligently for the young child.
When you have found him,
bring me the news so that I may go and worship him."
(Which the Wise Men might have done
had an angel
not intervened.)

Herod had the power, or so he thought,
to stop this new "King of the Jews" business
right in its tracks.
Kill the child.
How simple to plan;
how simple to do.
But the problem was
Herod did not know where to look.
For this "where" was not something a man like Herod could know.
This "where" only seemed to have an earthly address:
Bethlehem, in Judea.
Hard to find locations on a "cosmic" grid.
unless you are wise
or attentive to stars.

When the wise men left their audience with Herod,
there was the star,
as if waiting
to lead them on.
And the wise men "rejoiced" at the sight.
The very next verse simply said,
"When they were come to the house
(not "stable" or "cave"),
they found the child
with Mary his mother.
(Joseph seemed to have gone off somewhere,
or taken a break
from wonder.)
The wise men saw the mother,
saw the child,
and "fell down" in adoration!

Here the mind stops
at the sight
of wise men
kneeling,
offering gifts.

Carolyn J Sweers

Herod,
having been greatly disturbed by what he had learned,
waited for the wise men to return
so he would know where to find
and kill
this new
"King of the Jews".

But the wise men did not come back.
They were warned in a dream.
They went home a different way.
Another angel intervention
with more still to come.

Joseph, too, had a dream;
a second one.
This one warned him of the threat from Herod
and said, in effect,
get out of town
and do it soon!
"Arise, and take the young child and his mother,
and flee to Egypt."
Go to Egypt, the angel said, and stay there
until I tell you
that it is safe to come back.
(Matthew 2:13)

When it became clear to Herod
that the wise men weren't coming back,
Herod knew he had a lot to lose.
He also knew, or so he thought,
what he could do about it;
how he could eliminate
what he perceived as a threat.
Lacking specific information about the child the wise men sought,
he came up with a solution
and that was to kill all the boy babies
born around the same time.
This dragnet of violence
would surely snare
the one that was feared;
this new
"King of the Jews."

Herod took matters into his own hands,
which is never a good idea,
if you are a player in a cosmic drama,
which Herod was.

Herod, not knowing that the one he sought was gone,
carried out his bloody plan.
For the sake of the one, many were slain:
"the slaughter of the Innocents."

(Try putting that
on a Christmas card!)

ADORATION OF THE SHEPHERDS

"And there were in the same country shepherds abiding in the field, keeping watch over their flock by night. Lo, the angel of the Lord came upon them, and the glory of the Lord shone around them: and they were sore afraid. And the angel said unto them, Fear not: for, behold, I bring you good tidings of great joy, which shall be to all people. For unto you is born this day in the city of David a Savior, which is Christ the Lord. And this shall be a sign unto you; Ye shall find the baby wrapped in swaddling clothes, lying in a manger. And suddenly there was with the angel a multitude of the heavenly host praising God, and saying, Glory to God in the highest, and on earth peace, good will toward men.

"And it came to pass, as the angels were gone away from them into heaven, the shepherds said one to another, "Let us now go even unto Bethlehem, and see this thing which is come to pass, which the Lord hath made know unto us." And they came with haste, and found Mary, and Joseph, and the babe lying in a manger. And when they had seen it, they made known abroad the saying which was told them concerning this child. And all they that heard it wondered at those things which were told them by the shepherds. (Luke 2:8-20, KJV)

THE SHEPHERDS

There were shepherds,
abiding in the field,
keeping watch over their flocks by night
when
all of a sudden
an angel appeared.
No, they weren't dreaming
but they must have wondered
if they were.
This was no ordinary passage of the night
with stars moving in patterns
across a dark sky.
Nothing like this
had any shepherd ever seen.
But because something has not happened,
does not mean it can't,
if God is involved.
And so it happened,
an angel appeared
and there was glory shining
everywhere.

Carolyn J Sweers

An angel appeared and the shepherds were "sore afraid"
(which means, scared shitless,
if you really want to know
the truth.)

A word about angels.
It is commonly thought that angels are nice,
figures of inspiration,
sign of God's care
who like to have
their picture
painted.

It was the poet Rilke who set me straight about angels:
Here is what he said about them
(in the second of his <u>Duino Elegies</u>
translated by A. Poulin, Jr.)

"Every angel's terrifying. Almost deadly birds
of my soul, I know what you are, but, oh,
I will sing to you!
If the archangel, the dangerous one behind the stars,
took just one step down toward us today: the quicker
pounding of our heart would kill us..."

Angels may seem very nice...
at a distance,
or safely consigned to a painting
or a detail in some old story.
But to meet one,
to actually meet one?
I don't wish it.
Do you?

The angel the shepherds saw
seemed to have been sensitized
to deal with humans.
"Fear not!"
the angel said
in words the shepherds understood.
"Fear not:
for, behold I bring you good tidings of great joy
and this news is for <u>all</u> people."

The angel went on to give details
about the blessed event:
"Unto you is born this day in the city of David
a Savior
who is Christ
the Lord."
Pretty "theological", this message,
especially for shepherds
but they "got it"
nevertheless.

The angel went on to say:
"And this shall be a sign unto you:
ye shall find the babe wrapped in swaddling clothes,
lying in a manger."

What kind of directions are these!
Bethlehem was a small town
but presumably there was more than one manger
in town.
Would the shepherds have to go to any house
that had a stable and ask,
"Excuse me,
is there a newborn child
lying in your manger?"
That might have been embarrassing,
and not too safe.
But God, who seems to think of everything,
when He makes a plan,
led the shepherds
directly to where
they needed to go.

The shepherds seemed to know beyond all human reckoning
that what was waiting for them in Bethlehem
was greater even
than meeting
an angel.

Carolyn J Sweers

What did the shepherds do when they got to Bethlehem
and found the stable
and the child?

So amazing was the event
that the shepherds,
normally a taciturn lot
who are not given to speaking
when silence will do,
these guys,
these angel-dazzled
outdoor guys,
wouldn't shut up.
They told everybody,
everywhere,
what they themselves
had seen and heard.
"And all they that heard it wondered at these things
which were told them by the shepherds."

(Dear reader,
are you not, by now,
wondering, too?)

There were others who kept vigil that night.
Blind men whose blindness
forced their vision inward
to a place
with its own dawn.

There were others, not mentioned in the text, who kept vigil,
who had long ago prepared a place in their hearts,
just in case,
the Promise was true.
There were others who kept vigil,
who got up in the night and looked out a window when they
heard what they thought was the cry of a baby, borne on the
wind, from a place so unfamiliar,
it was not on any map.
Was this, at last, the cry of God?

Carolyn J Sweers

Following the account of the shepherds' visit,
Luke adds this telling detail:
"Mary kept all these things,
and pondered them
in her heart."
And what things there had been:
— angel visits
—the recognition by the babe in her cousin's womb
—shepherds telling of angels.
What must she have thought about
as she held the child?
What must she have wondered
as she watched him sleeping
and saw him reach out
as if to grasp
something she herself
could not quite see.

A SHEPHERD REMEMBERS

Sometimes I remember a night when
the sky caught fire
and light came down
as angel song.

Singing, just singing.
That was all there was...at first.
It was as if the words in some old book
had risen up,
and turned to song.
Only singing, it seemed, could let the grandness of the message
through.

Even now,
I cannot say
what it all meant.

We shepherds, half-crazed with light,
did what the angel said and followed the star.

We were held in the grip of the moment
when God was born.

Something was born in us that night.
Because, even though we were afraid, more afraid,
than we had ever been before,
we trusted the star.
We did not doubt
that this was where God
came to earth.

Carolyn J Sweers

WHAT DOES ALL THIS MEAN?
THESE STORIES OF ANGELS, AND KINGS AND BIRTHS?

What does all this mean,
you might ask.
May that question
keep luring you
until you, too,
find
the Holy Child.

Some night,
may angel songs
disturb your sleep
and send you out
into the dark
where
Radiance is found
in unexpected places.

A MEDITATION ON ADVENT

A TIME WHEN WAITING IS SACRED

This is the season of Mystery
made manifest.

A time to set our clocks
on inward time.

Carolyn J Sweers

The barns are full now
and the granary door is shut against marauding cold.
Earth lies
Hard as stone.
What means this
wintry time?
This time of waiting;
when lamps must be lit
at dawn.

What means
these darkened days
when those
who think they know
where they are going
stumble in confusion
while some lost travelers
find their way.

This is the time when eyes are drawn
to some Eastward point
in expectation
of new births.
This is a time of trusting
that it is not too late
to wait
for God.

Advent is a **waiting** time.
The people in the Christmas stories waited:
Zacharias waited
for the birth
that would bring
back the speech
his doubting lost.
His wife, **Elisabeth**, waited
as pregnant women must,
for the special one within her,
growing toward its birth.

Mary waited,
pregnant, too.
Mary, the receptive vessel,
said, while she waited,
'My soul doth magnify the Lord,
And my spirit hath rejoiced in God my Savior.
For he hath regarded the low estate of his handmaiden:
for, behold, from henceforth all generations shall call me
blessed."
Has there ever been a WAITING
as glorious
as this?

**Advent is a time to practice
not expecting in our usual ways.**

We have a long-practiced habit
of projecting our wishes
against some inner screen
and calling it "reality".
We make expectations
in our image.
What is expected, then,
is rarely
God.

One must be empty
and receptive
to wait for
the Lord.

What sort of waiting is this Advent time?
A waiting no longer tethered to imagined hopes.
A waiting near the wellsprings
of our deepest hopes.

Just being there,
with the not having,
with the not yet,
is an Advent task.

Have the courage to wait,
in reverent
expectant
silence.

**"Be still
and know."**

How hard that is--
both the silence
and the knowing.

In the beginning was the Silence,
the womb of the Word.
Before there was sound or ear to hear it,
there was Silence.

To be silent is to let go.
In the letting go
a Fullness comes.

How much trust it takes, to be silent,
how much faith:
**"the substance of things hoped for;
the evidence of things not seen"?**

Silence is more than
the absence of words.
Silence is the open space
where listening is.

Let our silence
be the speech
that calls.

O blessed Silence,
where no words impose a veil
to hide our hearts.
Speak to us of wisdom.
Speak to us of God.

Seed your word in us, O Lord.
Send us into empty places,
far from crowds.
Help us feel
the touch
of cosmic winds.
Help us see
deep darkness
glow.

If we did not venture into the dark night,
we might not find
the stable door
that opens
for a glimpse
of Wonder's birth.

We might fail to hear
the sound of angel wings
beating back
the dark.

Are you ready for the veil to lift?
Ready to be drawn toward wonder?

Those are the questions
an Advent season asks.

"In the beginning was the Word
and the Word was with God,
and the Word was God.

And the light shined in the darkness;
and the darkness comprehended it not.

The true Light...was in the world,
and the word was made by him,
and the world knew him not.

But the time came when
the Word was made flesh,
and dwelt among us,
and we beheld his glory."
(John 1 KJV)

What we had know as light before
was is in THIS light
a kind of dark.

For a moment, just a moment, the Word comes to us from far away.
　　Not just the far reaches of the time in which the prophet spoke,
　　　　but the further reaches that is the stern but benevolent,
　　　　action of God.
This news comes to us from some great distance
　　and for a moment,
　　it is enough,
　　　　to kindle hope.

For a moment, just a moment,
　　some ears of the previously deaf
　　　　will be opened to the astounding news,
　　　　　　that the very stuff of history,
　　　　　　　　stirred by fire and gentle force,
　　　　　　　　　　has come to new birth,
　　　　　　　　　　　　in a Bethlehem manger.

Word by word
　　phrase by phrase
　　　　the message must crowd out
　　　　all that prevents it
　　　　　　from being heard.

The vigil that is Advent:
Waiting, with a lighted lamp of awareness,
with darkness pressing round on every side.
Darkness within; darkness without.

To those who prepare their hearts,
some miracle has already taken place:
God's cradle, waiting and ready.
The dawning of the light
no darkness can put out.

Practice believing this
until you know.

It is not impossible!
It has happened!

CPSIA information can be obtained
at www.ICGtesting.com
Printed in the USA
FSHW022215010519

9 781949 746952

Encountering Christmas

This book is an attempt to defamiliarize the Christmas stories found in the Bible. Familiarity can result in a diminishment of wonder at the astounding news that God was manifest as a baby in a manger and that the event was announced by angels. The Christmas story is not about something that happened once. It has profound implications for understanding our own divine origin and task. That is why letting oneself be drawn into the stories as if for the first time can work wonders. Enter and see.

Carolyn Sweers grew up on an Iowa farm in the 1950's. It was there that she had her first experiences of the profound Silence she tries to describe in this book. These experiences, more than any others, shaped her life and led her to a career as a philosophy student and teacher. This book and others that she has had published recently, have a shared objective: to evoke insight in the reader. She knows from experience the importance of finding what Kierkegaard called "the truth for me." And, she shares the Socratic conviction that people have within them this truth. It simply needs to be revoked. That is what this book attempts to do.

LETTRA

ISBN 978-1-949746-95-2

90000

9 781949 746952